OCEAN LIFE UP CLOSE

Sea Anemones

by Mari Schuh

BLASTOFF! READERS

3

BELLWETHER MEDIA • MINNEAPOLIS, MN

Note to Librarians, Teachers, and Parents:

Blastoff! Readers are carefully developed by literacy experts and combine standards-based content with developmentally appropriate text.

Level 1 provides the most support through repetition of high-frequency words, light text, predictable sentence patterns, and strong visual support.

Level 2 offers early readers a bit more challenge through varied simple sentences, increased text load, and less repetition of high-frequency words.

Level 3 advances early-fluent readers toward fluency through increased text and concept load, less reliance on visuals, longer sentences, and more literary language.

Level 4 builds reading stamina by providing more text per page, increased use of punctuation, greater variation in sentence patterns, and increasingly challenging vocabulary.

Level 5 encourages children to move from "learning to read" to "reading to learn" by providing even more text, varied writing styles, and less familiar topics.

Whichever book is right for your reader, Blastoff! Readers are the perfect books to build confidence and encourage a love of reading that will last a lifetime!

This edition first published in 2017 by Bellwether Media, Inc.

No part of this publication may be reproduced in whole or in part without written permission of the publisher. For information regarding permission, write to Bellwether Media, Inc., Attention: Permissions Department, 5357 Penn Avenue South, Minneapolis, MN 55419.

Library of Congress Cataloging-in-Publication Data

Names: Schuh, Mari C., 1975- , author.
Title: Sea Anemones / by Mari Schuh.
Description: Minneapolis, MN : Bellwether Media, Inc., 2017. | Series: Blastoff! Readers. Ocean Life Up Close | Includes bibliographical references and index. | Audience: Ages 5 to 8. | Audience: Grades K to 3.
Identifiers: LCCN 2016035482 (print) | LCCN 2016042997 (ebook) | ISBN 9781626175730 (hardcover : alk. paper) | ISBN 9781681032948 (ebook)
Subjects: LCSH: Sea anemones–Juvenile literature.
Classification: LCC QL377.C7 .S36 2017 (print) | LCC QL377.C7 (ebook) | DDC 593.6–dc23
LC record available at https://lccn.loc.gov/2016035482

Editor: Christina Leighton   Designer: Brittany McIntosh

Printed in the United States of America, North Mankato, MN.

Table of Contents

What Are Sea Anemones?

Sea anemones are ocean animals. Their **tentacles** sway in the water like colorful plants.

They usually live on rocky coasts, **coral reefs**, or the ocean floor.

Species Spotlight
GIANT GREEN ANEMONE

life span:
up to 150 years

depth range:
0 to 49 feet
(0 to 15 meters)

giant green anemone range =

N W E S

conservation status: least concern

Extinct	Extinct in the Wild	Critically Endangered	Endangered	Vulnerable	Near Threatened	Least Concern

Sea anemones have **algae** living inside them. The algae help give the anemones bright colors.

Anemones are often pink, green, yellow, or blue. There are more than 1,000 types of sea anemones!

Soft Sea Creatures

Sea anemones do not have bones. They have soft, tube-shaped bodies.

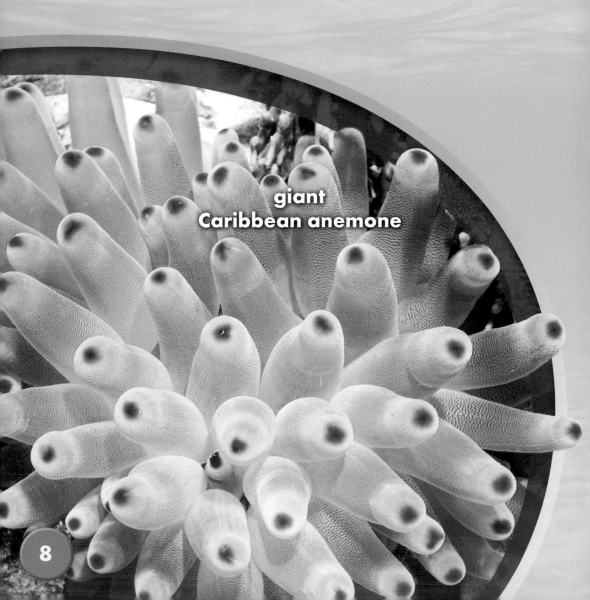

giant Caribbean anemone

tube anemone

Some sea anemones are thick and short. Others are long and thin.

The bottom of a sea anemone's body has a sticky foot. It attaches to rocks, **corals**, or shells.

Identify a Sea Anemone

soft body

tentacles

sticky foot

Sea anemones usually stay in the same spot. But they can move slowly using their foot.

Sea anemones are many sizes. Some are very tiny. These are only 0.5 inches (1.3 centimeters) across.

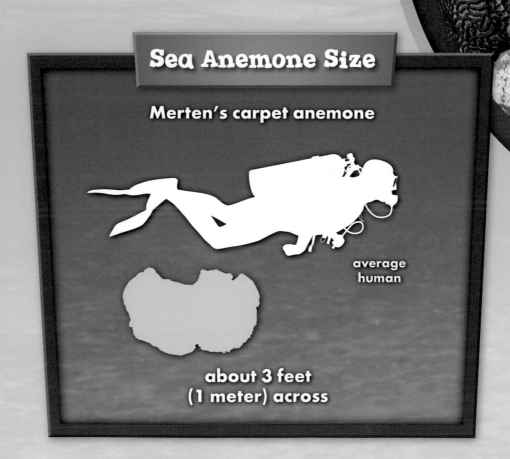

Sea Anemone Size

Merten's carpet anemone

average human

about 3 feet (1 meter) across

Merten's carpet anemone

Sea anemones can also be huge.
They can be more than 3 feet
(1 meter) across!

Food and Young

Sea anemones are **carnivores**. These **predators** wait for **prey** to swim by. Mussels and **zooplankton** are favorite foods.

Sea anemone tentacles sting prey with **venom**. Then, the anemone pulls the meal into its mouth.

Catch of the Day

zooplankton

blue mussels

red
sea urchins

eggs

Sea anemones grow in different
ways. Some come from eggs.
The tiny young anemones grow
after they **hatch**.

Other sea anemones split into two parts. Each part becomes a sea anemone!

Working Together

Sea anemones form friendships with other ocean animals. Their bond with clownfish is the most well known.

They protect each other from predators. Clownfish also eat **parasites** off sea anemones. In return, the sea anemones share their leftovers.

Sea Enemies

copperband butterflyfish

loggerhead sea turtles

leather sea stars

cloak
anemone

Some sea anemones live
on hermit crab shells.
When the crab eats, the
anemone gets scraps
of food.

The anemone helps protect the crab from enemies. Sea anemones and their friends work together to stay safe!

beadlet anemone

Glossary

algae—plants and plantlike living things; most kinds of algae grow in water.

carnivores—animals that only eat meat

coral reefs—structures made of coral that usually grow in shallow seawater

corals—the living ocean animals that build coral reefs

hatch—to break out of an egg

parasites—living things that survive on or in other living things; parasites offer nothing for the food and protection they receive.

predators—animals that hunt other animals for food

prey—animals that are hunted by other animals for food

tentacles—long, bendable parts of a sea anemone that are attached to the body

venom—a poison a sea anemone makes

zooplankton—ocean animals that drift in water; most zooplankton are tiny.

To Learn More

AT THE LIBRARY
LaPlante, Walter. *Sea Anemones.* New York, N.Y.:
Gareth Stevens Publishing, 2016.

Magby, Meryl. *Sea Anemones.* New York, N.Y.:
PowerKids Press, 2013.

Rake, Jody Sullivan. *Sea Anemones.* Mankato,
Minn.: Capstone Press, 2017.

ON THE WEB
Learning more about sea anemones
is as easy as 1, 2, 3.

1. Go to www.factsurfer.com.

2. Enter "sea anemones" into the search box.

3. Click the "Surf" button and you will see a
   list of related web sites.

With factsurfer.com, finding more
information is just a click away.

Index

The images in this book are reproduced through the courtesy of: Rich Carey, front cover, p. 4; Sphinx Wang, p. 3; Stas Moroz, p. 5; Randimal, p. 6; Holger Wulschlaeger, p. 7; Seaphotoart, p. 8; Tatjana Kabanova, p. 9; ligio, p. 10; David Havel, p. 11 (top left, bottom); Gertjan Hooijer, p. 11 (top center, top right); WaterFrame/ Alamy, p. 13; Lebendkulturen.de, p. 15 (top left); Kuttelvaserova Stuchelova, p. 15 (top center); Joe Belanger, p. 15 (top right); Norbert Wu/ Minden Pictures/ Getty Images, p. 15 (bottom); Age Fotostock/ Alamy, p. 16; Jeff Mondragon/ Alamy, p. 17; Vladimir Wrangel, p. 19 (top left); Natursports, p. 19 (top center); Greg Amptman, p. 19 (top right); Julia Belikova, p. 19 (bottom); Nature Photographers Ltd/ Alamy, p. 20; Andrey Nekrasov/ Alamy, p. 21.